W9-ATF-103

DATE DUE

15198

979.1
Tho

Thompson, Kathleen.

Arizona

STECK-VAUGHN
PORTRAIT OF AMERICA

Arizona

Steck-Vaughn Company

Executive Editor	Diane Sharpe
Senior Editor	Martin S. Saiewitz
Design Manager	Pamela Heaney
Photo Editor	Margie Foster

Proof Positive/Farrowlyne Associates, Inc.
Program Editorial, Revision Development, Design, and Production

Consultant: Don Harris, Director of Communications and Research, Arizona Department of Commerce

Published by Raintree Steck-Vaughn Publishers, an imprint of Steck-Vaughn Company.

A Turner Educational Services, Inc. book. Based on the Portrait of America television series by R. E. (Ted) Turner.

Cover Photo: Window Rock by Arizona Office of Tourism.

C.1 1997
15.98

Library of Congress Cataloging-in-Publication Data

Thompson, Kathleen.
    Arizona / Kathleen Thompson.
       p.   cm. — (Portrait of America)
    "Based on the Portrait of America television series"—T.p. verso.
    "A Turner book."
    Includes index.
    ISBN 0-8114-7323-6 (library binding).—ISBN 0-8114-7428-3 (softcover)
    1. Arizona—Juvenile literature. [1. Arizona.] I. Title. II. Series:
Thompson, Kathleen. Portrait of America.
F811.3.T46 1996
979.1—dc20
                                         95-38250
                                         CIP
                                         AC

Acknowledgments
The publishers wish to thank the following for permission to reproduce photographs:
P. 7 Arizona Office of Tourism; p. 8 © Russ Finley; p. 10 (top) Arizona State Parks, (bottom) Salt River Project; p. 11 Arizona State Parks; p. 12 Arizona Historical Society; p. 13 Arizona Office of Tourism; pp. 14, 15, 16 Bisbee Mining and Historical Museum; p. 17 Arizona Historical Society; p. 18 Magma Copper Company; p. 19 (top) Salt River Project, (bottom) © Ed McCombs/Navajo Community College; p. 20 (both) Jerome State Historic Park, Arizona; pp. 21, 22, 24, 25 Arizona Office of Tourism; p. 26 Petrified Forest National Park/National Park Service; p. 27 (top) Arizona Office of Tourism, (bottom) Arizona Cotton Growers Association; p. 28 Arizona Cattle Growers' Association; p. 29 (top) Arizona Historical Society, (bottom) Arizona Cattle Growers' Association; p. 30 Arizona Office of Tourism; p. 32 (top) Buffalo Bill Historical Center, (bottom) Arizona Office of Tourism; p. 33 Arizona Office of Tourism; p. 34 Scottsdale Center for the Arts; p. 35 © Bennie M. Gonzales Photo; p. 36 © Diane Gonzales; p. 37 (both) © Bennie M. Gonzales Photo; pp. 38, 39 © Superstock; p. 40 © Harvey Lloyd/Gamma Liaison; p. 41 © Superstock; p. 42 Arizona Office of Tourism; p. 44 National Optical Astronomy Observatories; p. 46 One Mile Up; p. 47 (left) One Mile Up, (center, right) Arizona Office of Tourism.

STECK-VAUGHN

PORTRAIT OF AMERICA

Arizona

Kathleen Thompson

A Turner Book

RSVP

RAINTREE
STECK-VAUGHN
PUBLISHERS
The Steck-Vaughn Company

Austin, Texas

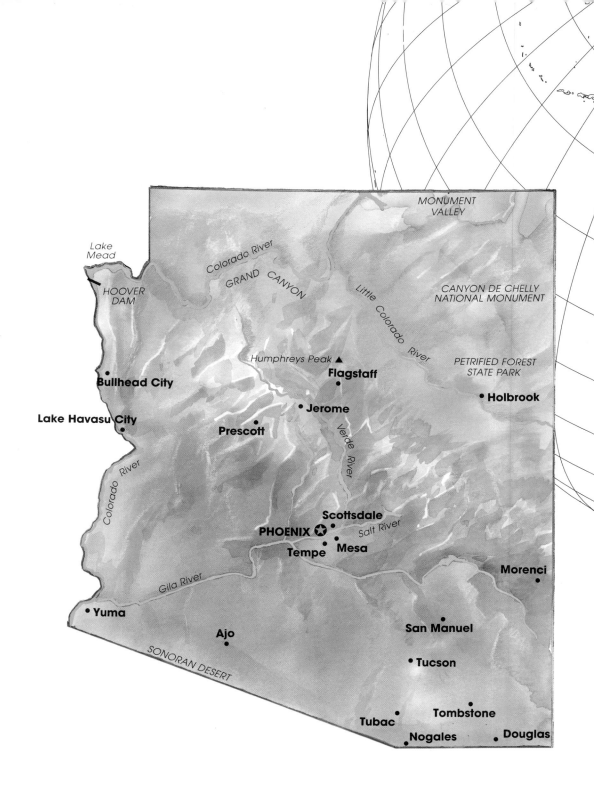

Arizona

Lake Mead

HOOVER DAM

Colorado River

GRAND CANYON

MONUMENT VALLEY

Little Colorado River

CANYON DE CHELLY NATIONAL MONUMENT

Humphreys Peak ▲

Flagstaff

PETRIFIED FOREST STATE PARK

Bullhead City

Holbrook

Jerome

Lake Havasu City

Prescott

Verde River

Scottsdale

PHOENIX ✪

Salt River

Tempe   **Mesa**

Morenci

Colorado River

Gila River

Yuma

Ajo

San Manuel

SONORAN DESERT

Tucson

Tubac

Tombstone

Nogales   **Douglas**

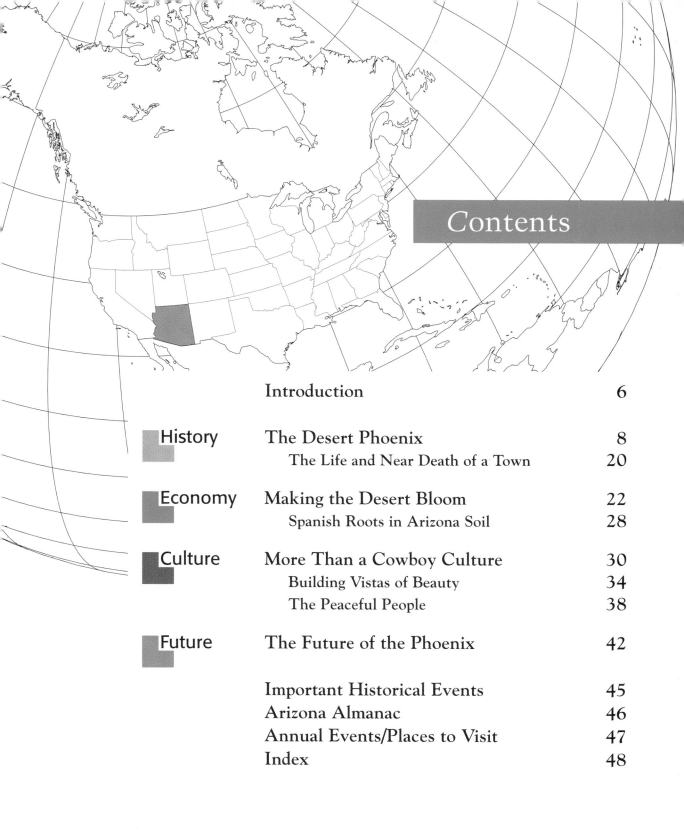

Contents

Introduction

Years ago most Americans thought of Arizona as a desert wasteland. But time has brought big changes—and huge population growth—to Arizona. Irrigation systems were put in place to pipe water to its soil. What had been desert became rich farmland. In the 1950s one invention changed Arizona forever—air conditioning! Arizona's population rose by five hundred percent between 1950 and 1990. People began to see Arizona as a tourist attraction. And the tourists haven't stopped coming to this place of painted deserts, petrified forests, and grand canyons. What was once thought to be a wasteland is now one of the nation's most visited places.

Vacationers enjoy rafting down the Colorado River, which runs through the Grand Canyon.

Arizona

The Desert Phoenix

In Greek mythology the phoenix was a bird that lived for five hundred years and then burned itself on a fiery altar. When the fire died down, the phoenix was born again from its own ashes. The Native American civilizations that lived in present-day Arizona began again like this mythical bird.

Archaeologists have found traces of human civilization in the Arizona desert that date back to 300 B.C. That is when Native Americans called the Hohokam lived on this land. The name *Hohokam* comes from the Pima and means "all used up." The Hohokam were a highly sophisticated people. They diverted the waters of the Gila and Salt rivers to irrigate their fields, using more than 150 miles of irrigation ditches. They grew cotton, corn, squash, and beans. They made beautiful pottery and intricate jewelry of shells inlaid with turquoise. Archaeologists have found what seems to be an observatory used by the Hohokam to chart the courses of the sun and the moon.

The Hohokam built this structure in the year 1350. It is now Casa Grande Ruins National Monument. The structure was probably used for observing the stars.

The figures on this rock were made by the Hohokam people. The Hohokam were skilled at many forms of art, including painting, pottery, and possibly even epic poetry.

The Hohokam civilization lasted for over a thousand years. About A.D. 1100, other Native American groups came from the north and lived peacefully among the Hohokam. By 1450 the villages were abandoned. Archaeologists are unsure why this happened. The villages may have been deserted because of changes in climate or because of war. The descendants of the Hohokam, the Tohono O'odham and the Pima, began anew in the areas once farmed by the Hohokam.

Anasazi culture in present-day Arizona dates as far back as 100 B.C. The name *Anasazi* is a Navajo word meaning "the ancient ones." Archaeologists have divided the Anasazi culture into separate periods—Basket Maker and Pueblo. The Anasazi built numerous communal dwellings, or pueblos, over a vast area of the Southwest. This area spread over the Four Corners region where today Arizona, Colorado, New Mexico, and Utah meet. Some of these dwellings were caves built into cliffs. Early Anasazi

The Hohokam lived in Arizona well over two thousand years ago. Many of their irrigation ditches, such as the one in the background of this painting, have been incorporated into water irrigation systems of today.

houses were made from logs and mud built over shallow holes dug in the ground. Later, about A.D. 1100, they built above-ground houses of stone and clay brick. The Anasazi disappeared more gradually than the Hohokam did. Although scientists are not sure why, there probably were many reasons. Some possible reasons include raiding groups, drought, famine, and internal quarrels among the Anasazi. Hopi, Zuni, and Rio Grande Pueblo peoples are direct descendants of the Anasazi.

In the 1500s, Spanish explorers came to this continent looking for gold to take back to Spain. Stories began to reach the Spanish in Mexico of seven golden cities to the north called the Seven Cities of Cíbola. The Spanish explorer Álvar Nuñez Cabeza de Vaca

During the years 700–1100, the Anasazi created *kivas,* or underground rooms, such as the one shown here. Kivas were used for ceremonies as well as for socializing.

came to this area in 1536. A few years later, Father Marcos de Niza, a Franciscan priest, came with a party led by Estéban, a former African slave. This group passed through the San Pedro Valley in 1539 looking for the golden cities.

Of course, they didn't find the seven cities. But Marcos de Niza claimed that he had seen them on the horizon. The famous explorer Francisco Vásquez de Coronado believed the story. The next year Coronado headed north to continue the search and passed through Arizona. The dwellings of the Pueblo people were the closest he found to the cities of gold. He abandoned his search when he reached the Grand Canyon.

It wasn't until about a hundred and fifty years later that Europeans came to Arizona to stay. In 1692 Father Eusebio Kino, a Jesuit priest, came into the area and explored much of the state. He established 24 missions in the Santa Cruz and San Pedro valleys. The missions in Arizona were not simply churches. The priests of the missions were representatives of the Spanish government. It was their job to convert the Native Americans not only to Christianity but also to the Spanish culture. They taught the Native Americans the Spanish language. Some Native American groups simply ignored the Spanish. In many cases, however, the age-old culture of a people was lost and replaced by Spanish culture.

Around 1736 the Spaniards began calling the area *Aleh-zon*, which means "little spring." It is derived from the Pima village of that name and later came to be pronounced "Arizona." In 1752 the first European

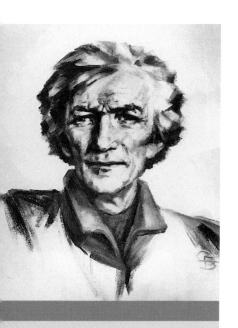

Father Eusebio Kino founded the original San Xavier mission in the early 1700s, almost a century before the famous mission building was constructed.

settlement in the area was founded at Tubac. It was a *presidio*, or fort, built by the soldiers.

In 1776 the soldiers were transferred to Tucson. Soldiers lived with their families inside the fort. The Apache who lived in the area resented the presence of soldiers. Battles between the two groups broke out continuously.

By 1821 the people of Mexico had won their independence from Spain. All of the area in the Southwest that had been claimed by the Spanish was now considered part of Mexico. By this time American and French frontier miners, settlers, and traders had begun to come into the area. Large United States settlements developed in parts of what is now the Southwest. The new settlers in these areas did not want to be governed by Mexico.

San Xavier del Bac mission in Tucson is called the "white dove of the desert." It was built in the late 1700s to carry on Father Kino's mission well after his death.

Cowboys, such as this young man from Arizona, came to symbolize the United States throughout the world.

In 1846 Mexico and the United States went to war. When the war ended in 1848, Mexico agreed to a treaty that gave the United States the Southwest, which included most of Arizona. In 1853 the United States acquired the rest of present-day Arizona in the Gadsden Purchase.

There were a lot of people in the country who didn't think the government had made a very good deal. The land, after all, was just desert, and they thought it was not good for much of anything. They called it the Wild West. But settlers came to Arizona anyway. It was rough country, peopled by cowboys, outlaws, and Native Americans. The Apaches were still fighting for their land. This struggle had been going on for nearly one hundred years!

In the 1850s, before the Gadsden Purchase, Arizona settlers had asked Congress to make Arizona a territory of the United States. That request was left unanswered. In 1861 the Civil War began. Many of the settlers in Arizona were from the South. They were sympathetic to the Confederate cause. In 1863 the Confederacy granted them what Congress had not. It declared that Arizona was now the Confederate Territory of Arizona. Confederate troops tried to gain control of the area in April 1862. They were soundly defeated by Union troops. But the declaration by the Confederacy prompted Congress to take action. Later that same year, Congress welcomed Arizona into the Union as an official territory of the United States.

The first capital of the Arizona Territory was Fort Whipple. In 1864 the city of Prescott was founded, and the capital was moved there. Finally the capital was moved to Phoenix in 1889.

During this time many farms and ranches were settled. More and more, Native Americans found their land taken over by settlers. The United States government began a policy to force all Native American groups onto certain areas, called reservations. Kit Carson, a scout whom the Native Americans had trusted, was hired to drive the Navajo from their land. The Apaches, led by Mangas Coloradas, Cochise, and Geronimo, struggled hard to regain their homeland from settlers. Geronimo finally surrendered in 1886, effectively ending Apache hopes.

In 1877 silver was discovered at what later became the town of Tombstone. Lawmen such as Wyatt Earp, Doc Holliday, and Bat Masterson came to the town around 1881. The town had a population of about seven thousand at that time. Arizona had a few other

The Apache chief Geronimo is on the horse on the left. He lived peacefully with settlers until a group of them killed his wife and children in 1858.

15

boomtowns that sprang up because of silver and gold discoveries. Copper mines in the 1880s and 1890s brought even more settlers.

In 1883 the Southern Pacific Railroad was completed. It ran from Los Angeles, passing through Tucson and Yuma before connecting with New Orleans. That same year workers completed the Atchinson, Topeka, and Santa Fe Railroad. This route cut across northern Arizona on its way from California to St. Louis. These railways opened up many new possibilities for trade with other states.

In 1910 Arizona was at last allowed to apply for statehood. The people of Arizona drafted a constitution, but President William H. Taft turned down their application. The reason was that the proposal had a clause in it that would allow Arizona voters to remove their judges from office. The people of Arizona took the clause out, and in 1912 Arizona finally entered the

The copper industry remained crucial to the development of Arizona from the mid-1800s until about 1950.

The Theodore Roosevelt Dam, the world's tallest masonry dam, was completed in 1911. It harnesses the power of the Salt River for electricity.

Union as the forty-eighth state. Then the new Arizona legislature simply put the clause back into their constitution. Arizona was the last of the contiguous, or connected, states to gain statehood.

One of the most important steps taken in those early days of statehood was the building of dams. Starting with the Theodore Roosevelt Dam, built on the Salt River in 1911, these dams provided irrigation, electrical power, and water for new cities. The newest phoenix was rising strong and healthy in the Arizona desert.

Due to improved mining methods, miners were getting more copper out of the ground. The copper-mining industry boomed. There were major strikes at Clifton and Morenci in 1915, at Jerome and Ajo in 1916, and at Bisbee in 1917.

The state began to call itself the land of the "five C's": copper, cattle, cotton, citrus, and climate. As more land was irrigated, agriculture expanded. Cattle

The Morenci open-pit copper mine is one of the largest in the nation. It measures almost two miles across.

ranches thrived, and the climate brought tourists, many of whom decided to stay. During the Great Depression of the 1930s, people all over the country left their homes looking for work, and many of them came to Arizona. During World War II, air bases were built in the state. Veterans who had been stationed in Arizona came back later with their families.

But the people who had been in Arizona longest were not full participants in the new state. It was not until 1948 that the state's Native Americans won the right to vote. In that year the Supreme Court of Arizona ruled that the sections of the state constitution that kept Native Americans from voting were illegal.

In the 1950s and the 1960s, Arizona began to change. Manufacturing became more important than mining and agriculture in the state's economy. Visitors who came to enjoy the warm weather and beautiful scenery made tourism an important industry. With all these new people, it became clear that the state would need more freshwater. In 1963 the United States Supreme Court ruled that Arizona was entitled to water from the Colorado River. In 1968 Congress authorized construction on the Central Arizona Project. This system of pumps and canals delivers water from the Colorado River to Phoenix and Tucson.

Things began to improve for Native Americans in Arizona, too. Some of the groups began to operate businesses and factories. Some others opened up parts of their reservations to paying visitors. Navajo Community College opened in 1969. It was the first college ever built on a reservation.

In 1988 the Arizona State House of Representatives voted to impeach Governor Evan Mecham for official misconduct. Later that year the state senate convicted him and removed him from office. Governor Mecham was only the seventh governor in United States history to have been impeached. Rose Mofford succeeded Governor Mecham, becoming Arizona's first woman governor.

Arizona is a technological wonder grown up from the desert. Its water is mostly imported. Its system of roads, airports, and railroads allows people to pass in and out of the state in ease and comfort. Air conditioning, computers, and other technology have helped create a kind of manufactured "indoor" world. But outdoors the Arizona landscape, with its vast panoramas, is full of color and drama. This combination of modern technology and natural wonder makes Arizona one of the most memorable states in the nation.

This canal gate is radio-controlled from a central location.

Navajo Community College is located in Tsaile, at the northeast end of Canyon de Chelly National Monument.

The Life and Near Death of a Town

Three prospectors who were searching for copper around the Verde River in Arizona found what they were looking for in 1876. They staked their claims and dug for copper until 1883. That's when Eugene Jerome and the United Verde Copper Company came and started a town named Jerome. The town was rich in copper deposits, and Jerome's population grew quickly. It was a boomtown.

Herb Young came to Jerome in 1911. He remembers the excitement of living in a boomtown. He also remembers that living was not easy. "The streets were unpaved and crossing a street during rainy weather was quite an adventure. You'd be apt to lose your shoes."

Working conditions for the miners were dangerous. Many men lost their lives in the mines. Blasting accidents and cave-ins were common. Even worse, there were no medical facilities. But the people kept coming. By the 1920s, Jerome had a population of more than 15,000 people.

Then the mines began to run out of copper. In 1953 the United Verde Copper Company closed the last mine

This saloon was part of the Boyd Hotel at the time Jerome was a boomtown. The hotel was first opened in 1899 and today houses a fudge store and a pottery shop.

This photo was taken at the corner of First and Main streets in the early 1900s.

Jerome is built on Cleopatra Hill, above the copper mines that made it a boomtown.

in Jerome. The company that had started Jerome also finished it off. The population fell to about fifty within a few years. Jerome was a ghost town.

In the 1960s some artists and craftspeople from the larger cities rediscovered Jerome. These people were looking for an affordable and quiet place where they could work and live. Many of them had dreamed of opening shops of their own. Jerome had many abandoned houses and shops that just needed a little fixing up. Soon more and more of these artisans arrived, and a community began to form. Richard Martin was one of the first members of this community. "We either jumped in to help get it together or the town would fall apart," he remembers. "Jerome came back to life because of the efforts of individual people doing their own things."

By the mid-1970s, Jerome was a small but thriving community of just over four hundred writers, musicians, craftspeople, historians, and artists. With the support of the original fifty residents, they brought Jerome back to life. Today the town is registered as a national historic landmark. It isn't a boomtown, but it's still growing. It took a strong commitment and a lot of cooperation from its modern-day residents to bring Jerome into its second century. There's no reason why it shouldn't enjoy a few more centuries.

Making the Desert Bloom

Arizona is a perfect example of what modern technology can accomplish. People in Arizona have gone into the desert and, where there was no water, they have brought water in by damming nearby rivers. Where the heat was uncomfortable or even dangerous for people, they have put in air conditioning. Technology has made Arizona what it is today. In return, Arizona has become one of the great centers of technology.

The industries we call "high tech" are different from the industries of the past. Other industries, such as oil and coal, are tied to a particular area because that area is where the resource is. High-tech industries are not tied to a particular area. In high-tech industries, the resources are people. They need people who are highly trained, with special skills. High-tech industries choose locations that will be attractive to the people they need. Many of these industries have chosen Arizona.

The first of these high-tech companies to choose Arizona was Motorola. This industry giant moved into

Phoenix International Raceway is a good example of the modern side of Arizona. Drivers race Indy cars and stock cars around the raceway, the world's fastest one-mile oval.

The Navajo are famous for their colorful woven rugs, such as the ones being sold here at a roadside stand.

the state in the early 1950s. Motorola now employs twenty thousand people in Phoenix alone and even more in other parts of the state.

Manufacturing accounts for only 13 percent of Arizona's gross state product. Yet it is still the state's single most important industry. The three major products manufactured in the state are transportation equipment, electrical equipment, and machinery. Over ten percent of the employed people in the state work in manufacturing. Almost half of those manufacturing workers make high-tech products. These include computers, solar cells, lasers, and equipment for airplanes, satellites, and space vehicles.

The fastest-growing industries in Arizona, as in most of the nation, are service industries. These are industries that do not make an actual product. Instead they do work for people or serve them in other ways. Service industries in Arizona include hotels, food stores, and government jobs. The government, in fact, either maintains or owns almost three quarters of Arizona's land. This means that there are plenty of service industry jobs at public schools and at state or national parks. There are also jobs in the service industry on Native American reservations and on military bases. As a whole, Arizona's service industries employ almost 450,000 people.

The Grand Canyon is Arizona's main tourist attraction. One of the Seven Wonders of the World, it is a mile deep, 277 miles long, and took more than two billion years to form.

Arizona relies heavily on its tourist industry. Visitors bring over $7 billion a year into Arizona. That amount has nearly doubled since the mid-1980s. Over 250,000 people are employed to serve the millions of tourists every year. They come to swim, ski, camp, and stand at the edge of the mighty Grand Canyon.

The next two largest industries—agriculture and ranching—together employ about 2.5 percent of the state's workers. Cotton has always been the most important crop, but citrus fruits and many vegetables and grains are also plentiful. Farms and ranches are larger in Arizona, on average, than in other states. But bigger does not always mean better. This relatively

Petrified Forest National Park in northeastern Arizona is one of the state's areas where further development is not allowed.

small industry uses almost ninety percent of the state's precious water supply.

Copper mining, part of what started the state on its way to economic success, has steadily dropped off since the 1950s. Mining now employs less than one percent of working people in Arizona. The state still supplies almost three quarters of the nation's copper, however. And it still boasts the nation's largest underground copper mine, at San Manuel.

Arizona has one of the three largest Native American populations in the country. There are more than 160,000 Native Americans living in the state. Their twenty reservations cover an area about the size of West Virginia. The treaties that guaranteed these lands for Arizona's Native Americans also guaranteed housing and education. Those promises have not always been kept. Poverty levels on reservations are some of the worst in the nation. For Arizona's Native Americans, there is another equally important problem. It involves the constant struggle between preserving a traditional way of life and living in the modern world.

Many Native Americans have made ends meet by managing agriculture and ranching industries. Others run factories, restaurants, hotels, service stations, arts and crafts stores, and other businesses. Most reservations also sell Native American arts and crafts. Many

Many sheep ranchers prefer to maintain traditional ranching methods instead of adopting modern techniques.

others also charge tourists who want to observe their traditional ceremonies.

Arizona has thrived economically for most of its history, and its high-tech base should keep it flourishing. But all this development has its price. Increasing pollution and decreasing water levels are taking their toll on the state's natural beauty. The Native Americans have learned to adapt in a modern high-tech era. So, too, will Arizona's high-tech industries need to find a way to bring in the new age, while preserving its natural resources.

This cotton picker helps keep Arizona's cotton yields among the nation's highest.

Spanish Roots in Arizona Soil

The Aguirre family can trace their roots back to Spain in the 1500s. Since 1852, when the family moved to the United States, they've been cattle ranchers. Enrique Aguirre remembers, "Years ago, all we did was mostly cattle business, when my father was in his prime. We had a ranch where we had probably 18,000 to 20,000 acres of land, . . . about 8,000 head of cattle, and many, many horses."

Enrique is proud that his family still ranches. But the industry has changed. For one thing, family ranches have gotten much smaller. Today the Aguirres' ranch, called Red Rock, keeps a base of only 250 cattle. Enrique had to take on farming to supplement the ranching income. His son Rick increased farming to approximately one thousand acres. Rick hopes to start a full-fledged ranch resort on the land. In fact, he may have to if he wants Red Rock to keep making money.

Things are very different now than they were in the early days of the Aguirres. To round up the cattle, trucks are also used instead of just horses. Meanwhile, the family's Spanish tradition is beginning to fade, as relatives go into other businesses and marry people of different backgrounds.

But the Aguirres have kept two main parts of their heritage: their cattle and their close family ties. Enrique's brother Yjinio Aguirre is a

These cattle are grazing on the open range in the heart of Arizona cattle country.

Arizona cowboys copied the clothing of Mexican vaqueros, or cowboys. They wore sombreros and bandanas.

historian of Spanish cattle culture. To him, family is the most important part of Spanish culture. "Well, I believe the Spanish tradition is a very beautiful tradition," he says, "because the people are very close. . . . In our family, I was forty and was still under my father's wing."

That part of life has not changed for the Aguirres. They hope that it never will change. Rick's son and daughters are already helping him out on the ranch. "I wish we could all keep on living together," says Yjinio. "That's what my folks expected of us . . . to stay together." The shrinking cattle business is making this goal difficult for the Aguirres. But they've come this far, and with a little more luck and flexibility, Red Rock will carry on the family cattle business for generations to come.

The Aguirre brothers are branding a calf. Every spring ranchers brand calves with red-hot irons. A brand shows an imprint of letters or a symbol representing a particular ranch.

29

More Than a Cowboy Culture

At the beginning of this century, the world was hungry for stories of the American West. In the streets of eastern cities, people bought thousands of cheap novels about strong, silent men who sat tall in their saddles and were quick with a gun. In the refined parlors of New York and St. Louis, they thumbed through magazine stories about shootouts, cowboys, cattle rustlers, and Native Americans, some noble and some "savage."

The stories were often miles from the truth—and no wonder. Their authors were often miles from the West. But as writers moved from other parts of the country to Arizona, westerns became more accurate. One of the few western writers from that era whose works have survived is Zane Grey. Born in Ohio, he spent most of his life west of the Mississippi, writing about Arizona and other areas of the Wild West. His most famous book, *Riders of the Purple Sage*, was set in the Grand Canyon area.

Three members of the Clanton band were killed by Wyatt Earp and Doc Holliday in the famous shootout at the O. K. Corral in Tombstone. The gunfight occurred in 1881 and has inspired Western writers ever since.

Artist Frederic Remington also served as a reporter and illustrator during the Spanish-American War, in which the United States won control of most of Arizona.

The saguaro cactus grows larger than any other cactus in the United States and can be found in the Sonoran Desert in southern Arizona.

Many artists who drew or painted pictures of cowboys were also from other parts of the country. These artists, too, found their greatest inspiration once they settled in Arizona. Painter, sculptor, and illustrator Frederic Remington was born in New York, but he based much of his work on his experiences in Arizona and other western states.

Although many of Arizona's greatest cowboy writers and artists were not born in the state, one famous cowboy tradition was. The first organized rodeo was held in Arizona on the Fourth of July in 1888. It was called a "Cowboy Tournament" back then. Its tradition is now carried on yearly in Prescott.

Arizona's Native Americans are also a powerful part of the state's culture. Arizona's Native Americans create paintings, jewelry, cloth, baskets, and pottery. They use traditional methods to create their works of art. In this age of assembly-line production, people appreciate the Native Americans' handcrafted works.

Native American ceremonies are another unique art form that expresses their culture. These ceremonies combine dance, music, and elaborate costumes in celebrations of nature and Native American religions. The Arizona Navajo organize the largest of these ceremonial gatherings in the United States. Their five-day Navajo Nation Fair, held every September, attracts more than one hundred thousand people. Such fairs are open to the public. But almost all Native American groups, including the Navajo, have certain ceremonies that are only open to members.

Arizona has the most national parks and monuments of any state in the nation. The vast stretches of desert and the majestic mountain ranges have been a part of all of Arizona's cultures. You would have a hard time finding a song, painting, or story from Arizona that doesn't somehow reflect the impact of the landscape.

Arizona's many museums represent its diverse blend of cultures. Native American, Spanish, and cowboy museums are found all over the state. Some museums specialize in one of these traditions, but most combine all three.

Many of these museums, such as the Heard Museum and the Scottsdale Center for the Arts, are works of architectural beauty themselves. In fact, many different styles of architecture can be found in Arizona. Many buildings combine both the smooth-faced style of ancient Anasazi pueblos and the simplicity of the Spanish missionary buildings. The San Xavier del Bac Mission, located near Tucson, is a famous example of the Spanish style. This structure was built in the early 1700s. An example of more modern architecture is found in Taliesin West, the former home of Frank Lloyd Wright.

Arizona's culture reflects many styles, from traditional to futuristic. Its culture is a reflection of the state itself. Arizona is proud of its ancestry. It is a place where the past has a welcome place in the present.

Bull riding at the Page Rodeo is a popular event. A cowboy is required to stay on the bull for eight seconds.

Building Vistas of Beauty

Arizona is a state of open spaces and magnificent views. The sunlight is bright and hot. The desert winds sweep across plains and around rocky peaks. Some of Arizona's most beautiful buildings seem to match its landscape. Architect Bennie M. Gonzales designed many of these buildings.

Bennie Gonzales was born in Phoenix in 1924. His parents were also born there. His family combines German, Irish, French, Mexican, and Native American heritages—"Arizona potpourri!" as Mr. Gonzales says. His first years were spent on his father's ranch outside Phoenix. He got to know the Arizona land well in his youth, helping his family grow vegetables and raise chickens and livestock.

When Bennie Gonzales was seven, his father died. His family moved into Phoenix. Bennie's new neighborhood was called "Mexican Town." His neighbors were bricklayers and workers who built adobe houses. Adobe is a building material made

CENTER FOR THE ARTS

The Scottsdale Center for the Arts, which was designed by Mr. Gonzales, features theater, music, and dance performances, as well as art exhibitions.

Bennie Gonzales designed the Nogales Public Library at the beginning of his career. Nogales is actually two cities—the border between the United States and Mexico runs right through it.

from mud and straw. These traditional southwest buildings are distinguished by softly rounded corners. Bennie Gonzales believes that living in this neighborhood had a lot to do with shaping his career. As he says, "If you grow up making mud pies, it's hard to get it out of your system." Everyone in Mr. Gonzales's family worked in construction, too. His uncle, Santiago Cahill, was a contractor. He built

Arizona's Heard Museum and Camelback Inn.

Bennie Gonzales enjoyed going to building sites with his uncle. He spent many days sweeping floors and bringing the workers their tools. Mr. Gonzales admired the architects most. They designed the buildings, and they were respected by the workers. Mr. Gonzales's uncle encouraged him to become an architect.

In 1941 Mr. Gonzales joined the Coast Guard. For the next five years, he enjoyed traveling the world. Wherever he went, he studied architecture. He dreamed of designing wonderful buildings back home in Arizona.

Bennie Gonzales at last returned to Arizona and got a degree in architecture at Arizona State University. Then he studied in Mexico for a year. In 1958 he opened his own architecture office in Phoenix.

Mr. Gonzales had plenty of business. When he was asked to design the Nogales Public Library, however, he began to receive national recognition. He remembers all the planning that went into that project. There were so many things to think about! He kept

He painted his buildings in creamy colors, which he later called "Aztec white" and "Navajo white." He added stained glass on some buildings. This is the colorful glass found in the windows of some churches. He wanted the bright Arizona sun to "throw" colors into the rooms. He gave some of his buildings deep-set windows and sharp angles. No one had created such buildings before. And no other buildings seemed so right for Arizona!

Mr. Gonzales had his seventieth birthday in 1994. He has designed buildings as far away as Saudi Arabia and as close as California. His 36 years in architecture have brought him many awards and world fame. Bennie M. Gonzales, Inc., Architects, is the same company that he first started in 1958. Now, however, he has three architects, a landscaper, and three other professionals working for him.

Mr. Gonzales says his designs are borrowed from the colors and open spaces of the Arizona landscape. The

asking himself questions about the building he was to design: What was the need of the people? What materials were available? Who was actually going to construct the building? What would be the best material for them to handle? He still asks these same questions on every new project.

Bennie Gonzales brought new ideas to architecture. He recreated the look of adobe using concrete and stucco, a decorative plaster material.

people of Arizona certainly believe that his architecture fits well in the desert. The state has been one of his biggest customers, spending more than twenty million dollars on his buildings. Mr. Gonzales's architectural career is slowing down. He's glad to have time for his other interests, though, such as painting. "Now that I have more freedom," he says, "I enjoy architecture more than ever." He hopes that future generations take architecture as seriously as he has. "If we plan wisely and well," he says, "our cities can be vistas of beauty."

The St. Elizabeth parish church in Sun City features Gonzales' creamy white plaster and stained glass windows.

Mr. Gonzales designed this Navajo Reservation Hospital, located in Chinle.

The Peaceful People

In the northeastern part of Arizona is an area occupied by a very special people. They are called the Hopi, which is a word that means "peaceful people." Theirs is one of the oldest cultures in the United States. They began settling in the area around the year 1100. Their reservation is over a million-and-a-half acres of settlements, farms, and ranches.

The government estimates their population at about ten thousand, but they are such a private people that no one is sure.

The Hopi live on and around *mesas,* or isolated hills with flat tops. This means that most of them live at about five thousand to six thousand feet above sea level. The mesas were crucial to the Hopi in the early days of their civilization. The steep sides of these land formations protected their villages from Navajo and Apache raids.

Walpi, a Hopi mesa village, was built at the edge of a cliff. It is still inhabited and has existed for centuries.

This woman has almost finished weaving a sewed coiling basket. She weaves the bundle of fibers into a coil and then sews each coil to the one below it with a needle. Sewed coiling is a basketry technique over five thousand years old.

Today there are three mesas within the Hopi reservation. The reservation's twelve villages are concentrated around these areas, which they call First Mesa, Second Mesa, and Third Mesa.

The Hopi have always been a deeply religious people. Their religion takes a lot of commitment. They try to live in harmony with the land and with each other. They are mostly farmers in a harsh, dry climate. Rainfall is scarce, so many Hopi religious ceremonies involve prayers for rain. Throughout the year, the Hopi have celebrations with ceremonial dances. Some of these celebrations are open to the public.

Some of the ceremonial dances begin just after sunrise. In the cool air of the morning, the drums begin to sound, steady and rhythmic. The dancers move slowly and gracefully to the beat. They are dressed in traditional ceremonial outfits. The drumbeats quicken, then slow once again. The effect is hypnotizing. Many spectators stand still for hours just watching. The dances go on throughout the day.

For outsiders, getting to see one of these ceremonies is often a matter of luck. These dances are religious events for the Hopi. The date for each one is determined by the village according to its customs and traditions. The village might announce an event only a few days before it is to take place. Although the public is usually allowed in, some villages close their ceremonies to outsiders.

These Hopi posed in their traditional outfits before taking part in a public ceremony.

Sometimes several villages hold ceremonial dances on the same day. Then visitors can spend time at each village watching parts of several dances. Every non-Hopi visitor, however, must get permission from each village leader to attend a ceremony. Photographs, recordings, or even sketches of either the ceremonies or the villages are strictly prohibited.

Other Hopi ceremonial dances are private celebrations and may be closed to non-Native Americans. Kachina dances, which take place from January to July, are closed to the public in ten of the twelve Hopi villages. The Hopi believe that kachina are ancestral spirits that help them communicate with their god. They perform kachina dances to help or protect a harvest, bring rain, or help the community in other ways. In these colorful ceremonies, dancers wear masks and elaborate costumes. If the ceremony is performed correctly, the Hopi believe that the dancers themselves are temporarily transformed into the kachina spirits. Most Hopi groups believe in more than five hundred different kachina spirits. A different ceremony is performed to summon each of these spirits.

Another private Hopi ceremony is the snake dance, which is usually performed every August. This ritual takes nine days to perform. What happens during the first eight days is kept secret. The Hopi help maintain this secrecy by performing the ceremony in underground rooms called *kivas*. On the ninth day, ceremonial dancers perform with live snakes.

Some Hopi have left the three mesas. They look for jobs in the cities and attend universities. But they do not hide any part of who they are. They carry with them the spirits of the kachina and the name that means "peaceful people."

This Hopi kachina doll is standing next to a pottery plate. Kachina dolls are made to look like kachina spirits. Children play with kachina dolls to learn what different kachina spirits look like.

The Future of the Phoenix

The future of Arizona depends on water. It's that simple and that complicated. Arizona today uses some of the irrigation ditches built by the Hohokam people. Some look at this as a positive sign, saying that they are learning important lessons from earlier cultures. Others see such connections as linking the fate of Arizona's residents to the mysterious fate of the Hohokam. Can the water last forever?

Arizona's legislators point to the 1991 completion of the Central Arizona Project, a program conceived in 1968. Miles of pumps and canals now connect the Colorado River to the Phoenix and Tucson area by means of this system. Legislators boast that this project will ensure Arizona's water supply far into the twenty-first century. But many forget that the water of the Colorado must be shared with many other desert states in the Southwest, including the crowded Los Angeles area and the rest of southern California. On top of that, the underground water table, another crucial source of Arizona's water, has dropped as much as

Arizona's high country is home to elk, deer, and bears, as well as the largest ponderosa pine forest in the United States.

250 feet in some places since 1945. There are conservation efforts in Phoenix and Tucson now that are designed to deal with this problem.

Such worries are easy to overlook in the face of all of Arizona's positive signs for the future. The state economy is thriving. The high percentage of high-tech industries should ensure its continued health. In fact, the first half of 1994 alone brought 177 new businesses or business expansions to the state.

Another promising area for the future of Arizona is the study of astronomy. Thousands of years ago, the Hohokam studied the movement of the sun and moon. Today, Tucson is the official Astronomy Capital of the World. It has a higher concentration of telescopes than any other city. Kitt Peak has the largest solar telescope in the world. Pluto, the farthest-known planet in our solar system, was discovered by astronomers working at the Lowell Observatory in Flagstaff. Such technology will certainly help to secure future prosperity.

But Arizona's high technology doesn't free it from modern problems such as pollution. Industry and development are taking their toll on Arizona. This state used to be a "clean-air" resort for people with respiratory problems, but the air is now threatened by pollution. As the population booms, Arizona's beautiful landscape is threatened more and more. What the future of Arizona needs more than anything else is vision that comes from the wisdom of the past.

The Kitt Peak Observatory contains 18 telescopes. It sits atop a 6,875-foot mountain on the Tohono O'odham Reservation, southwest of Tucson.

Important Historical Events

300 B.C.	The Hohokam culture develops in central and southwestern Arizona.
200	The Mogollon culture develops in southeastern Arizona.
100	The Anasazi culture develops in northern Arizona.
A.D. 1539	The Franciscan priest Marcos de Niza claims present-day Arizona for Spain while looking for the Seven Cities of Cíbola.
1540	Another Spanish explorer, Francisco Vásquez de Coronado, goes as far into Arizona as the Zuni River. A part of his group reaches the Grand Canyon.
1692	Eusebio Kino, a Jesuit priest, founds the Guevavi Mission.
1752	The first Spanish fort is built near Tubac.
1776	A fort is built in Tucson.
1821	Mexico becomes independent of Spain, making Arizona part of Mexico.
1846	The United States goes to war with Mexico.
1848	The treaty that ends the war with Mexico gives the United States all the area north of the Gila River. This includes most of Arizona.
1853	The United States acquires the southern part of Arizona from Mexico as part of the Gadsden Purchase.
1854	The first copper mine is opened at Ajo.
1862	Union forces defeat Confederate forces in Arizona, but the Confederacy claims Arizona anyway. Then Congress claims the Arizona Territory for the Union.
1864	Arizona's capital is moved to Prescott.
1867	The capital moves again, this time to Tucson.
1877	Arizona moves its capital yet again, back to Prescott. The Southern Pacific Railroad reaches Arizona.
1886	Organized Native American attacks in Arizona end when Geronimo surrenders.
1888	The nation's first organized rodeo is held at Prescott.
1889	Arizona's capital moves to Phoenix.
1911	Work is completed on the Theodore Roosevelt Dam.
1912	Arizona enters the Union as the 48th state.
1936	The Hoover Dam is completed.
1948	Arizona recognizes the right of Native American citizens to vote.
1963	The United States Supreme Court apportions water from the Colorado River to various states, including Arizona.
1965	Lorna Lockwood is appointed to the state supreme court, making Arizona the first state with a woman chief justice.
1968	The Central Arizona Project, a plan to supply Phoenix and Tucson with more water, is approved by Congress.
1971	London Bridge is moved from the Thames River in London to the resort town Lake Havasu City in Arizona.
1981	Sandra Day O'Connor, an Arizona judge, becomes the first woman appointed to the United States Supreme Court.
1991	The Central Arizona Project is completed, improving Arizona's water supply.

45

The blue in the Arizona flag symbolizes liberty, just as it does in the United States flag. Red and yellow rays represent the brilliant colors of the Arizona sky every sunrise and sunset. The 13 rays symbolize the original colonies of the United States. A copper star in the middle of the flag stands for the copper mining that first brought people to Arizona.

Arizona Almanac

Nickname. The Grand Canyon State

Capital. Phoenix

State Bird. Cactus wren

State Flower. Saguaro cactus blossom

State Tree. Paloverde

State Motto. *Ditat Deus* (God Enriches)

State Songs. "Arizona March Song" and "Arizona"

State Abbreviations. Ariz. (traditional); AZ (postal)

Statehood. February 14, 1912, the 48th state

Government. Congress: U.S. senators, 2; U.S. representatives, 6. State Legislature: senators, 30; representatives, 60. Counties: 15

Area. 114,007 sq mi (295,276 sq km), 6th in size among the states

Greatest Distances. north/south, 389 mi (626 km); east/west, 337 mi (542 km)

Elevation. Highest: Humphreys Peak, 12,643 ft (3,855 m). Lowest: 70 ft (21 m)

Population. 1990 Census: 3,677,985 (35% increase over 1980), 24th among the states. Density: 32 persons per sq mi (12 persons per sq km). Distribution: 87% urban, 13% rural. 1980 Census: 2,718,425

Economy. *Agriculture:* cotton, hay, beef cattle, citrus fruits, lettuce. *Manufacturing:* transportation equipment, electrical equipment, machinery. *Mining:* copper, gold

State Seal

State Flower:
Saguaro cactus blossom

State Bird: Cactus wren

Annual Events

★ Winter Carnival in Alpine (January)

★ Gem and Mineral Show in Quartzsite (February)

★ Gold Rush Days in Wickenburg (February)

★ Cinco de Mayo Mexican Celebration in Tubac (May)

★ Wyatt Earp Days in Tombstone (May)

★ Frontier Days and Rodeo in Prescott (Fourth of July)

★ Apache Tribal Fair on the Fort Apache Reservation (September)

★ Navajo Nation Fair in Window Rock (September)

Places to Visit

★ Apache Trail in Tonto National Forest, near Apache Junction

★ Grand Canyon National Park

★ Heard Museum in Phoenix

★ Kitt Peak National Observatory in Tucson

★ London Bridge in Lake Havasu City

★ Meteor Crater, near Winslow

★ Montezuma Castle National Monument, near Camp Verde

★ Navajo and Hopi Native American villages in Navajo County

★ O.K. Corral in Tombstone

★ Petrified Forest National Park and Painted Desert, near Holbrook

★ San Xavier del Bac Mission in Tucson

Index